WHAT I WISH I KNEW
WHEN I STARTED
YOUTH MINISTRY

STUPID MISCONCEPTIONS, AND CARING FOR YOUR OWN SOUL WHILE MINISTERING TO OTHERS

MIKE YACONELLI &
MARK OESTREICHER

WHAT I WISH I KNEW WHEN I STARTED YOUTH MINISTRY

Youth Specialties

www.youthspecialties.com

Youth Specialties

What I Wish I Knew When I Started Youth Ministry
Copyright © 2000, 2005 by Youth Specialties

Youth Specialties Products, 300 South Pierce Street, El Cajon, CA 92020

Unless otherwise indicated, all Scripture quotations are taken from the Holy Bible: New International Version (North American Edition). Copyright © 1973, 1978, 1984 by International Bible Society. Used by permission of Zondervan.

Some of the anecdotal illustrations in this book are true to life and are included with the permission of the persons involved. All other illustrations are composites of real situations, and any resemblance to people living or dead is coincidental.

Web site addresses listed in this book were current at the time of publication. Please contact Youth Specialties via e-mail (YS@YouthSpecialties.com) to report URLs that are no longer operational and replacement URLs if available.

Creative Team: Jay Howver, Laura Gross, David Conn
Cover Design: Holly Sharp
Printed in the United States of America

05 06 07 08 09 10 / CHM / 10 9 8 7 6 5 4 3 2 1

INSIDE...

For 35 years Youth Specialties (YS) has worked alongside Christian youth workers of just about every denomination and youth-serving organization. Each year YS serves more than 100,000 youth workers worldwide through training seminars and conventions, resources, and the Internet. YS aims to train and encourage youth workers so they can effectively reach and guide adolescents to authentic Christian faith.

MY STUPID MISCONCEPTIONS

Mark Oestreicher

For a second I thought I'd broken her neck. And in my selfish immaturity, my first reaction was not whether Barb was okay, but rather how her screaming was drawing negative attention my way.

It was my second week as a 19-year-old youth ministry intern for my home church—a large church with a thriving youth ministry. I was at a beautiful camp in northern Michigan, with about 50 high school students, preparing the facility for its upcoming summer of ministry. And we had an afternoon break to swim in the frigid waters of Lake Huron.

Barb was a junior in high school and a major flirt. But hey, her flirting affirmed me, so I flirted back. When I picked her up and put her over my shoulder, I was proving (in my own mind) what a stud I was, what a cool guy I was, and how all the students on the trip could relate to me as a peer. I jogged out into the cold water with Barb folded over my shoulder, her playful screams drawing just the kind of attention I wanted.

But the water didn't get deep fast enough, and I got tired of carrying her. So I dropped her—in about a foot of water—on her head.

After the crying stopped and the afternoon wound down, the youth pastor sat me down and said (I still remember every word 17 years later), "Well, Mark, so far you've pretty much blown it."

That event was the dawn of my realizing I didn't have everything figured out. Even after growing up in a killer youth ministry and going off to college to be trained for youth work, I had a boatload of misconceptions about youth ministry. And it took years and lots of dumb moves to uncover and overturn them.

Really, I wasn't an absolute idiot. At least no more incompetent than the next 20-year-old, overly confident, semi-cocky youth worker.

If you're fortunate, you've already debunked the misconceptions I learned about the hard way. But just in case you're still hanging onto any of these stupid misconceptions, let's name them and do our best to lose them.

MISCONCEPTION:

MY ROLE AS A YOUTH WORKER IS TO BE A BUDDY TO THE STUDENTS.

If I can get the kids to see me as their buddy, then they'll open up their lives to me, I thought. Well, it worked—unfortunately. That summer, as an intern I had a bunch of spiritually marginal kids treat me like a buddy. But there was a wee problem: it put me in a position of impotence. I had earned their confidence, but I hadn't earned a place of authority in their lives, the right to speak to issues from a godly perspective. I was just one of them—no more. Ministry-wise it was a total dead-end.

I remember John; he was just a sophomore, but he acted much older. He had a quiet confidence that made him way cool. I admired his self-assurance and hung out with him, hoping to gain his favor, to get an in with him. It wasn't all about my wanting to be accepted—I wanted to have a spiritual impact on John, though I had absolutely no idea how I would do this or what it would look like. I listened to—and laughed at—John's off-color jokes, maybe making an "oh, behave" face occasionally. I compromised to win his trust, and I got it. He trusted me enough to let me into his life. But I had absolutely no spiritual impact on his life. None. Zip. Maybe even a negative impact.

The role of the youth worker is not to be a buddy or a pal. If you hang out with teenagers all the time and see them as peers and best friends, something is wrong with you and you shouldn't be in youth ministry. Sure, you'll befriend kids. But you're their leader, and that defines you as a different kind of friend. Yes, you'll hang out and talk about things other than Jesus. But your relationship with students, as chummy as it may seem at times, needs to maintain the foundational understanding that your reason for hanging is not to be a pal—it's to have a spiritual impact on their lives.

MISCONCEPTION:

I SHOULD IDENTIFY AND CONFRONT ALL THE SIN IN STUDENTS' LIVES.

Once I wiggled and manipulated my way into the closest confidence of students, I figured, then I could address their deepest and darkest sins. The flaw in this thinking wasn't in my ability to find out their deepest and darkest sins. The flaw was in thinking this was good ministry.

Face it—I was trying to be the Holy Spirit. How stupid is that? I continue to meet 30- and 40-year-old youth workers still laboring under the false assumption that it's their job to convict students of sin.

Not that you shouldn't confront sin. You should. But it's not your primary role. Leave God's work to God.

Later during that same summer I dropped Barb in the lake, the youth pastor detected this misconception in me and sat me down again. He said something like this: "The kids don't need a lighthouse on wheels, rolling around and shining light into all the dark corners of their lives. They need a lighthouse on a rock, consistently beaming its light in the same direction, dependably and predictably, so that as they scurry around, they have a consistent point to look to, a predictable beacon of light as a reference point."

This analogy changed the way I do one-on-one youth ministry. Yes, I challenge kids. Yes, I confront sin regularly. But my perspective is different. I see that my primary influence will not be in challenging or confronting but in setting a consistent example of Christ living in me.

MISCONCEPTION:

I CAN FIX ANY STUDENT.

With enough time, with the right mix of fun interaction and spiritual challenge, and with my brilliant kid-magnet relational skills, I was sure I could schmooze my way alongside any kid and then bring them into a deep walk with Jesus Christ. I wasn't silly enough to believe I could do this with *every* kid, but I did think I could handle any individual teenager you threw my way.

Trevor was a high school junior and fairly popular at his school. I don't remember why he began attending our youth group—he really didn't fit in. Trevor was into breakdancing and so was I (it *was* the early '80s, after all). And I used that shared interest to strike up a relationship with him. It was a good start. But no matter how much time I spent with Trevor, no matter how good an example I was, no matter how much I challenged him, no matter how many youth group events Trevor attended—he didn't seem to change much. Maybe a little. But I'd be surprised if I found out he was walking with God today.

And you know what? Trevor's failure to "go for it" with God isn't a reflection of my failure as a youth worker. I don't know why Trevor didn't experience a major lifestyle change and develop passionate allegiance to Christ. Hey, there were kids I barely noticed then who are missionaries today. The Holy Spirit works in teens' lives in different ways and with different timing. And teens respond to the Holy Spirit in different ways. My part of this equation is, frankly, quite small.

I need to be faithful to represent Jesus Christ to teens. How they respond is not in my control.

MISCONCEPTION:

I'VE GOT TO BE COOL, PLAY GUITAR, AND SPEAK THE LINGO.

Oh yeah, baby, that was me. I was the funky-fresh youth meister. Knowing I was heading into youth ministry, I asked my parents for a guitar for high school graduation. When I became a youth worker, students probably thought I was semi-cool occasionally. Most of the time they probably thought I was a pathetic loser.

I still struggle with this misconception. And my probability of successfully pulling off "cool" is decreasing by the day. But like many youth workers, I still want kids to think I'm cool. And it's easy to fall into the false thinking that being cool increases ministry effectiveness. It ain't necessarily so.

Matt was a volunteer youth worker at my last church, and he was also cool. Actually, Matt was the single biggest geek I've ever met. He was wrapping up a Ph.D. in theoretical chemistry—which isn't *real* chemistry (in my book), just computer simulations for playing what-if games about compounds and molecules. He was a full-on pocket-protector-wearin', plaid-pants-with-a-striped-shirt, rhythm-deficient, stereotypical dweeb. And he was one of the most effective youth workers I've ever met. He reached kids I would never reach. And not only computer geek future theoretical chemists. He loved on teens and stuck with them, and he was unapologetically himself. Students loved him, and they respected his authenticity.

Put-on hipness might get you some initial attention with students. But it won't take you very far. God's best gift to your ministry is you. And your best programming tool is you. Be yourself.

MISCONCEPTION:

PARENTS ARE THE PROBLEM—EVEN THE ENEMY.

Parents mess up their kids for 15 years and then expect us to fix them in a couple hours a week.

I've heard youth workers say this. I maybe even said it myself. It's an extremely seductive statement. One we can secretly believe.

Everyone knows that teenagers, by definition, are going through a time of individuation, gaining independence, and forming their own identities. It's rare that this doesn't cause at least some amount of tension between teens and parents. And because the job of parenting teenagers is such a tough one, most parents experience a mixture of success and failure. At least some of these failures are things you and I, as savvy students of youth culture, would not have made. (Actually, we would make a completely different set of mistakes— probably far worse.) It's easy to conclude that all the problems our students face are the result of poor parenting.

Now add the fact that you will undoubtedly have a few parents who'll make unreasonable demands of you. This misconception is the result. But here are some important facts to hang onto:

Fact 1: The number-one influence in teenagers' lives is still their parents. Multiple studies prove this is true.

Fact 2: Parents *do* have countless more hours of influence in their children's lives than you do.

Fact 3: Parents have the primary spiritual responsibility of raising their children and bringing them up in Christ. You don't have that responsibility.

These facts do not mean that all parents care about their children's spiritual well-being. And they don't negate the fact that many students are raised in oppressive and unloving home environments.

But I've seen it over and over again and have experienced it myself. Youth workers become more effective as they age and begin to come alongside parents, rather than trying to take the place of parents.

MISCONCEPTION:

ADVISORY TEAMS AND BOARDS ARE USELESS DRAGS ON YOUR MINISTRY.

I figured I knew a lot more about youth ministry than they did. And I was sure they just wanted to spy on me and place hurdles in my way. So I kept them in the dark. I patronized them with sanitized reports that would have impressed a political spin doctor. I asked them to make decisions but only about things I didn't care about.

So it should have come as no surprise that the youth council at my church turned on me. When I was facing some vicious elders and my back was against the wall, I needed the protection of the youth council—but it wasn't there.

I learned. At my next two churches, I created a parent advisory team and decided the only way they could really function was if I gave them power. I asked them to approve events and to set the prices. I asked them to approve our teaching schedule. I even told them, in detail, when I'd made poor decisions. It protected me big-time.

God's wisdom often emerges from the collective work of a team. Surround yourself with people you trust and then choose to trust them, even when it feels risky. Yup, you might get burned. But it's more likely you'll get saved when you're drowning. It's worth the risk.

MISCONCEPTION:

I'VE GOT BETTER IDEAS THAN OTHER YOUTH WORKERS.

I noticed a few other churches or youth workers who were running goofy programs, and I quickly became convinced that I was superior in my ability to think about youth ministry and generate great ideas. I'd visit the largest, most impressive churches around, and all I noticed was everything they were doing wrong.

This was, plainly, my arrogance. And I've found that it's a common attitude among youth workers, especially young ones.

Just this week I received an article from a young youth worker entitled, "Why Youth Specialties Must Change or Die." I welcomed the input—even handed out copies of it to others at YS, hoping to glean some insight about how we should evolve and grow. In the end, it was little except the spouting off of a 20-year-old youth worker who was supremely confident about his view of youth ministry and the world.

It may be a stereotype, but renegade and maverick types seem to be drawn to youth ministry. These people are inclined toward delusions of competence. But as you grow older in youth ministry—and in life—you'll do one of two things: You'll realize how little you know. Or you'll become an immature, self-inflated, 30-year-old clutching exhausted ideas and mere holograms of youth ministry.

Woody was a youth worker who realized how little he knew. I ran into him at the National Youth Workers Convention a few years ago. We had lunch together. The guy was humble with a sweet spirit that reflected Jesus Christ. He had been slugging away in youth ministry at the same church for a dozen years. The guy's a saint, another (though unknown) Mother Teresa or Billy Graham. I wish the youth ministry departments at Christian colleges and seminaries offered a course called "How to Be Like Woody."

MISCONCEPTION:

THE BEST CURRICULUM IS THE STUFF I WRITE.

Okay, I'll admit it. This is one misconception where I'm letting my bias as the publisher at Youth Specialties show.

It's really the arrogance monster (again). These are statements I hear all the time:

"I don't trust curriculum from publishers—I'd rather write my own."

"I've never found anything on this subject, so I wrote it myself." (This usually comes attached to a proposal for a book product that has a dozen look-alikes on the market already.)

Here's the deal: You may be able to write kickin' materials, but it will take you a long time—time that could be spent doing other ministry functions. And occasionally, you may teach a subject that is truly outside any resource available. But the reality is that good writers and good publishers have prepared stuff for your use in ministry, and much of it is good.

So a one-word modification to this misconception makes it a wonderfully true statement: *The best curriculum is the stuff I modify.*

I never teach straight out of a printed resource. Even the best curriculum writer doesn't know my students, my community, my church, or me. I've got to modify it.

MISCONCEPTION:

YOUNG ADULTS MAKE THE BEST YOUTH WORKERS.

You might have this misconception floating around in your mind—especially if you're under 25. But this isn't a misconception just for young youth workers. It's common in the church in general. It grows out of the notion that young adults relate best to kids and, after all, relating to students is what youth ministry is all about.

Don't get me wrong—young adults can make great youth workers. They're usually single and have more flexibility with their time and schedules. They're usually more energetic and can get in there and mix it up with students. They're usually much more in tune with current youth culture, since many of them are still a part of it. And they have the distinct advantage over older youth workers of still remembering what it was like to be a teenager.

But there's a flip side: a seasoned adult can bring maturity to youth ministry that younger adults may lack. Parents tend to trust older volunteers more. They have larger pools of life experiences to draw from when they make decisions about the welfare of kids, and they're more likely to have wisdom (again, because of more life experiences) when connecting with teens' deeper needs.

Maybe your experiences so far have helped you develop at least a cognitive commitment to team-based ministry. So I won't preach on that theme. Here's how I see it: to realize the most benefits from team ministry means there has to be diversity—diversity of genders, diversity of ages, and diversity of ethnic backgrounds.

A young-adult leader relates to students as an older brother or sister.

A 30-year-old leader often takes on the role of an aunt or uncle.

A middle-aged leader becomes a secondary parent figure.

And it's totally cool if you have some grandparent-types on your team too.

MISCONCEPTION:

OTHER CHURCHES ARE MY COMPETITION.

My first church was on the large size—about 700 people. Our youth ministry had about 80 kids. But our suburb also had two megachurches—both of them had well over 2,000 people with youth ministries in the hundreds. They had big budgets, interns, secretaries, and resources galore. I had a dinky little youth room, a joke for a budget, and access to very few resources. And we regularly lost students to the megachurches.

I was cordial with their youth pastors, and we even did some events together. But I was always trying to prove our worth as a youth ministry. I wanted them to send our kids back to us (but I rolled out the red carpet for any visitors from those churches).

What a waste of time, emotional energy, and thought. And what a sin.

There are plenty of students to go around. If teens get plugged in at another church—God bless 'em. Be true to your call, love the kids God brings your way, and don't fall prey to the American consumer mentality that says you're competing with other churches.

MISCONCEPTION:

THE GOAL IS TO BE BIG.

These days I'm a youth ministry volunteer, since my day job is helping other youth workers through Youth Specialties. I meet regularly with my church's 23-year-old junior high pastor. He's a great guy—full of confidence and natural ability. But like so many youth workers, young and old, he's got the numbers disease (a disease that even good ol' King David had).

We've got about 125 junior highers on an average Sunday these days—pretty big. But the junior high pastor recently communicated to the volunteer team that one of our goals is to have 700 junior highers within five years.

I've been needling and cajoling him about this dubious goal. It's completely unrealistic, for one thing. Worse, it's a lousy goal.

Sure, we want to reach as many kids as possible. Yes, we're compelled by Christ to take the gospel to students. But nowhere in Scripture do we get any inclination that God prefers a group of 700 kids over a group of eight. In fact, most of the stuff I find in the Bible seems to point just the other way: God wanted Gideon to have *fewer* men in his army...God sent Josiah to Jericho *without* large numbers or weapons...David got in big-time trouble for counting his troops.

Nothing will burn you out faster than being small and striving for large. Nothing will lead you to pride quicker than having a large group and focusing on that fact. Check out the story of Uzziah (2 Chronicles 26) if you need to know the result of pride.

MISCONCEPTION:

YOUTH MINISTRY IS THE MOST IMPORTANT MINISTRY IN THE CHURCH.

I absolutely love junior high ministry. I've devoted my life to young teen ministry. And for years I worked on the premise that junior high ministry is the most important ministry in the church.

I think part of this misconception was a martyr complex. ("Boo-hoo, no one understands young teen ministry, so I'll show them my ministry is superior.") Another part was insecurity. The only legitimate part of this misconception was passion—but even that was slightly misguided.

Passion is essential. And it's very important that you have a sense of calling about the importance and strategic nature of youth ministry. But use caution. It's easy to allow this good and important passion to mutate into arrogance. (There's that word again.)

For years, youth workers have thrown around the supposed fact that 80 percent of Christians make a decision for Christ prior to the age of 18. And we've liberally used this theory to pelt people with our conviction that youth ministry is the Billy Graham of all ministries. Unfortunately for this theory, new research shows that the new breaking point is prior to 14 years of age. And the bulk of these decisions are made in children's ministry. Let's just get off our high horse and take our rightful place among all the important ministries of Christ's bride.

I no longer believe youth ministry is more important than other ministries in the church. (I'm just glad God didn't call me to the parking ministry or library ministry.)

MISCONCEPTION:

SAFETY ISSUES ARE FOR OTHER PEOPLE AND OTHER CHURCHES.

I'd always heard how I should take a head count when the kids piled into the van or bus—*every* time. And on big trips with lots of kids, I did this. But I was sloppy on small trips with just the dozen or so kids.

Until, on a mission trip into Chicago, I lost a 13-year-old girl in a Southside neighborhood. At night.

On our way back to the semi-abandoned but secure apartment building that was our home away from home, we stopped for a snack at McDonald's. I had looked around to see if anyone was still in the restaurant when we were leaving, but hadn't counted or checked names. When we left, Laura was in the restroom.

She waited at the restaurant for a half hour, hoping I'd realize she was missing and come back for her. When it didn't happen—and since she was only five blocks from our apartment building—she proceeded on what became a walk of terror. Gang members shouted obscenities and threats at her. When she finally got to our building, she found the door locked.

Meanwhile, we were all safely situated up on the third floor. A student ran into my room to tell me Laura was pounding on the outside door. I still hadn't realized she was missing.

Every seasoned youth worker has hideous stories like this one—filled with broken bones and threatened lawsuits and near misses—because safety precautions seem tedious and unnecessary to inexperienced youth workers. So you take shortcuts.

Being meticulous about permission slips is a drag.

Creating bus rosters makes you feel like the Gestapo—and if you don't feel this way, students will suggest you do.

Volunteer applications and thorough screening seem so time-consuming when you need workers.

And face it, risky games are fun.

So you'll have to do what doesn't come naturally. You'll have to decide that the tedium, the red tape, the process, and the caution are worth it. At the risk of sounding like an old, finger-wagging geezer, I'll say the blunt and painfully obvious truth: you'll think safety issues are only for other youth workers until a lawsuit or a death affects your group.

MISCONCEPTION:

IF I IGNORE PROBLEMS, THEY'LL GO AWAY.

The church board had made a ridiculous request of me—wanting a formal written report about a personal issue that had no effect on my ministry. In truth, they were out of line to ask.

But I should have done one of two things: given them the report, or respectfully informed them where they could put their request.

But I chose to be passive-aggressive and ignored them. Bad choice. A year later they fired me.

There's no perfect church. In the best of churches, in the most ideal situations, you'll have problems—problems of your own making and problems thrust upon you. Ignoring them is a sign of immaturity. And the problems will only snowball. So walk through problems, not around them.

MISCONCEPTION:

A LOT CAN BE ACCOMPLISHED IN THE FIRST YEAR.

When you land in a church, you sense a high expectation. It's almost palatable heaviness—or maybe lightness—in the air, like everyone with any reason to give a rip about the youth ministry has just taken a deep breath and is waiting with expectant little grins on their faces. But no one is exhaling. You feel the pressure to perform, to get results. Quickly.

A youth worker rolls into town with a big bag of tricks—flashy events, mind-blowing stories, lots of razzle-dazzle. Well, the tricks run out. They can only be repeated so many times. So the youth worker says to herself, "I guess I've done everything I can at this church," packs up her neat bag of tricks, and, after 18 months moves on to the next expectant church.

You can create a lot of flash in the first year. But it won't last.

Check out Jesus. Even he didn't make a flashy appearance to start his ministry. In fact, he did very little ministry during the first of his three years. He performed almost no miracles, and the ones he did perform were on the private side. He didn't stand on mountainsides and preach to thousands—or even to 700 junior highers—that first year.

Instead, he built relationships.

So this misconception isn't exactly a misconception. The first year of your ministry in a church *is* vital, and so much can be accomplished. But it's seldom the flashy stuff.

After working in four churches, this is what I've discovered: that youth ministry didn't start humming, didn't get to the point where I was remotely content with what was going on, until my third year. It took that long to infiltrate the system with the vision and strategy God had given to me. It took me at least that long to build an effective volunteer team. (The best volunteers often hide for a couple years just to see if you're worth working alongside.) It took three years to build trust with parents and boards and the senior pastor. It took that long to know the culture of the community and the local church.

So relax. Give yourself some time. You still have to run a program, but focus on the foundational stuff—relationships, locating and building student and adult leadership, casting vision, and communicating values.

MISCONCEPTION:

EVENTUALLY I'LL HAVE YOUTH MINISTRY TOTALLY FIGURED OUT.

I see some older youth workers who, unfortunately, *do* think they have it figured out. They're often the ones who package their program and take it on the road. ("Here's how you should do youth ministry—just like me!") They're fit for this kind of sales job because they've lost their effectiveness with actual students.

The longer I stay in youth ministry, the more obvious it becomes how little I know. My growing awareness of how clueless I am about how and when God will work in students' lives is humbling.

Sure, you'll grow in your knowledge of ministry and students and the church. You'll sharpen your speaking, programming, and relational skills. You'll learn from failures and successes. You'll probably become quite proficient at being a youth worker, in time.

When I started in youth ministry, I was pretty sure I understood students and student ministry. After a year I thought I had it almost figured out. After a few years, I thought I understood a fair amount. Now, with my instincts and skills and philosophy and vision and understanding much more developed, I see how little I know and understand.

That's good news!

Youth ministry is always a challenge, is constantly changing, and is regularly surprising. •

CARING FOR YOUR OWN SOUL WHILE MINISTERING TO OTHERS

Mike Yaconelli

Everyone was saying that I was doing really well, but something inside was telling me that my success was putting my own soul in danger.

—Henri Nouwen, *In the Name of Jesus*

The call of God is difficult to explain but impossible to ignore. It is the nagging, conscious awareness asking you to do something. The asking comes not from words, but from deep within, as though a voice had been planted inside and, now, is beginning to speak. This voice, the calling voice, has many ways of speaking—your passion for young people, the unique parts of you that seem to attract young people, the sense of joy and fulfillment that overflows into your soul when you're with young people. It is the great YES of your life that fills you with a sense of belonging, the warmth of being home. Heady wine, this call to youth ministry.

The call of youth ministry is unmistakable, relentless, captivating.

And dangerous.

Because in reality, it is a job. And once ministry becomes a job, the rules all change, and Youth Ministry the Job conflicts with Youth Ministry the Call. Youth Ministry the Job has a job description, performance objectives, mission statements, evaluation forms. It's about measuring—how many, how much…growth, success, results.

Youth Ministry the Call, on the other hand, is a mystery—and (trust me) the mystery of youth ministry is very frustrating for church boards and executive pastors.

Youth Ministry the Call has a rhythm all its own—slow.

- Youth Ministry the Job is about wider. Youth Ministry the Call is about deeper.

- Youth Ministry the Job is about more. Youth Ministry the Call is about one.

- Youth Ministry the Job is about program. Youth Ministry the Call is about relationship.

- Youth Ministry the Job is about being in your office. Youth Ministry the Call is being wherever young people hang out.

- Youth Ministry the Job is about young people's souls. Youth Ministry the Call is about your soul.

I remember my first years of youth ministry. My reckless passion for young people, my burning desire to introduce young people to Jesus, my ego and arrogance—it all had a momentum all its own. It was the late '60s and the world was ready to bless anyone willing to help America's wayward and rebellious youth. I was anxious to get started, and my church was anxious for me to get started.

It never occurred to either my church or to me that something critical was being ignored—my soul.

Not much has changed. The urgency of young people's needs combined with the demands of program and expectations—these push youth ministers along at an ever increasing speed. As long as young people are showing up and parents are happy, no one—least of all the youth minister—is inclined to ask, "What price am I paying to keep this program moving at such a fast pace?"

The road I've traveled for the last 40 years is lined with the burned-out remains of youth workers who discovered too late the need to care for their own souls.

"Hey, my passion for God will never diminish," you say. "I'll never allow myself to reach the place where my soul is in danger."

I hope you're right. But my experience tells me our souls are *especially* in danger when we're in youth ministry. Youth ministry is a seduction. Once you've experienced how young people respond to you, listen to you, want to be like you—these make it very difficult to think about your soul. The instant gratification of relationships with young people drowns out the delayed gratification of a relationship with Jesus.

I wish someone had warned me about the hazards of youth ministry. I wish someone had sat me down and told me what they wished they'd known when they started out in youth ministry. I wish someone had flagged me down while I was rushing around fulfilling everyone's expectations. Of course, maybe they did, but I was going too fast to see them.

So after 40-plus years of youth ministry, I feel obliged to share what I've learned from my mistakes and to warn youth workers of the obstacles ahead. I mean, it took me fifty years to understand what intimacy with Jesus even meant. To the contrary, I spent most of my youth ministry years trying to prove to Jesus that I was worthy of his love by trying to impress him with all I was doing.

("Come on, God, tell me something else to do. What do you want me to do now?")

In *Stories Jesus Tells*, John Claypool writes about putting his four-year-old to bed, she took three trips to the bathroom, asked for a drink of water, wanted another story told, needed Dad to put the light on, heard sounds, and so on. When she was finally settled down, John retreated upstairs to write. He was deep into his writing when he sensed her standing at the study door.

He turned around. "Laura, what do you want me to do?" he asked with more irritation in his voice than he wanted to betray. She padded into the room and grabbed his arm.

"Nothing, Daddy. I just want to be close to you."

I was too long in youth ministry before I let myself hear Jesus whispering to me, "I don't want you to do anything right this minute—I just want to be close to you." I may have learned this a lot earlier if someone had told me then what I want to tell you now:

YOU ARE RESPONSIBLE FOR YOUR OWN RELATIONSHIP WITH GOD.

I still remember my first church and my first senior pastor, a man I admired. When I signed on, I looked forward to spending many hours with my new boss, talking about our faith and being mentored by this godly man. He was seminary trained, I was not. He had lived many years, I was very young. In fact, a big reason I took this job was the opportunity to learn from the wisdom of this pastor.

Talk about disillusionment. I never saw him. We hardly conversed; when we did, it was about some youth activity or an upcoming mission trip or the lock-in the next week. My pastor was distant, preoccupied, and seldom talked about his own relationship with Jesus.

Then there were staff meetings. After a string of "regular" jobs during college, I was eager to be among staff who talked about Jesus during their meetings.

Talk about disappointment. Each meeting began with prayer, but the remainder was all about the choir, the carpet, the building campaign, vacation Bible school, the parking lot, the budget, and the damage to Fellowship Hall after the latest lock-in. Seldom did we talk about the Bible or our relationships with Jesus. Even our prayers were typically about church business—at best, they were about church members who were sick or in need.

I had unconsciously counted on my pastor and staff to help me stay on track with Jesus. I expected the business of the church to be incidental to the Jesus of the church.

I couldn't have been more wrong. Though it sounds harsh, this was the truth of it: it took me a long time to realize that no one cared about my relationship with Jesus. Oh, they cared plenty if my dry soul caused me to run off with the organist. But when it came to routine business and weekly meetings, no one expressed any interest in my relationship with Jesus. *My relationship with Jesus was assumed.* It was up to me to keep current with Jesus. It was up to me to find time in my busy schedule to find time for God. It was up to me to struggle with my own faith. The institution simply expected me to come to work every day with my faith intact and current. Yes, our conversations carried the appropriate Godtalk. Yes, we often prayed about specific issues that had arisen in our church. Yes, we even talked about the Bible once in a while.

But it was clear that we were hired to do the work of the church. The work of the *soul* was to be done after hours, on my own time.

Which is actually good news, of course, because we *are* responsible for our own spiritual nurture and growth. If you're going to survive spiritually, then take charge of your own relationship with Christ—perhaps along these lines:

- Write into your job description TIME ALONE WITH JESUS. Ask for a day each week, or a weekend each month, or a week every six months, to be set aside for you to work on your soul. These days can be spent in solitude, silence, on spiritual retreat or prayer retreat—whatever it takes to *listen for God in your life.*

- Ask for a reading budget that's separate from your

budget for youth ministry books. Ask for money to buy books about the spiritual life—just for you, not to make lessons.

- Suggest the staff get together weekly or even daily for communion (that would be Eucharist) to help the staff remember their calls.

- Find yourself a wise, older person who will agree to meet with you regularly to help you listen to what God is saying in your life. (That would be a spiritual director.)

- Journal regularly. Journaling gets you in touch with your interior. Your writing often reveals a part of you that you weren't consciously paying attention to.

- Ask the staff to brainstorm ways to increase the percentage of time during staff meetings spent on their relationship with Jesus. (There will always be business to discuss, so be realistic.) If the staff now spends 90 percent of the time talking about business and 10 percent about their souls, see if you can get them to agree to 80/20; then later maybe even 70/30.

- Suggest the staff have annual (or monthly or semi-annual) spiritual retreats, during which time the only subject is their own relationship with God.

YOU ARE MORE IMPORTANT THAN YOUR STUDENTS.

Sounds selfish, I know. "Seek ye first the kingdom of God," you remind me. Yet you'll tend to spend all your energy on the spiritual life of your youth group kids. If you're like most youth workers, you'll gradually wear down to the point of reading the Bible primarily for ideas for your talks and lessons, rather than for your own relationship with God. If you're like most youth workers, your praying will tend to occur only during meetings or church events. Before you know it, you're living your spiritual life vicariously through others. You'll hear a sermon or read a good book, and you think only what a good talk illustration it'll make. When a teenager in your group makes a life-changing decision, that moment becomes a prop for your spirituality—rather than relying on your own decisions and your own moments.

If you want to avoid this terribly easy slide from Youth Ministry the Call to Youth Ministry the Job, then you'll have to remember we are not about fixing people or situations. We are about being with Jesus. The best gift you can give a young person is not to fix their problems, but to help them recognize the presence of a Jesus who will never leave them nor forsake them, even when their lives plod along unfixed.

When young people observe the unfixed, broken you and your relationship with God, they learn the power of their own relationship with God in the middle of their brokenness. If your youth ministry begins with *your* relationship with Jesus instead of theirs, then working on your own soul isn't periphery or extracurricular—it's central to your ministry. Your soul *is* your ministry.

Real ministry is not what you do, but who you are.

DON'T SPIRITUALIZE SPIRITUALITY.

Taking care of your soul does not mean retiring to a monastery.

Knowing that during the previous year my friend, Brennan Manning, had done numerous silent retreats (for varying durations—weekends, one week, 30 days), I guiltily confessed to him my embarrassment at how comparatively little effort I'd made at taking the time to be alone with God.

"Mike, quit being so hard on yourself," he told me. "You think about God all the time. That is prayer. Even now you are praying all day long. Just because I'm on a 30-day silent retreat doesn't mean I'm on my knees praying the whole time—I'm reading, walking, sleeping, watching birds, thinking about my next speaking engagement."

I didn't recognize my own relationship with God because I had put Brennan on a pedestal. I compared my life to his. And consequently, prayer became inaccessible to me. Whenever you compare what you don't know about someone else to everything you know about you, you lose. I couldn't be Brennan Manning, and I don't have to be. I *still* haven't been on a seven-day silent retreat. But what I have done over the years is find my own way of being with God.

Granted, my relationship with Jesus is erratic and irregular. I have periods of time where I read voraciously, pray a lot, and spend much time thinking about my Savior. Then there are dry, barren times when I wonder where God is. My irregular schedule has become a regular part of my life, and it works for me. I don't have a routine for my prayer life. I don't have routines for *any* part of my life. I'm not a routine kind of guy. What's important is to understand what kind of man or woman you are—and then be true to that person in your walk with God.

READ LIKE A MADMAN.

Most youth workers don't read. Yet reading is absolutely essential to your spiritual growth.

- Ask the people you admire and respect what books they read. If you're drawn to someone, chances are they have the same reading interests you do, so trust them to get you on the right track.

- Note those authors you resonate with, then get *all* their books. I have my own group of authors who, through their books, have become my reading-world friends: Eugene Peterson, Barbara

Brown Taylor, Walter Wangerin Jr.,
John Claypool, Earl Palmer, Henri
Nouwen, Calvin Miller, Frederick
Buechner, Alan Jones, Will Willimon,
Evelyn Underhill, and Phillip Yancey. I
read everything they write. Somehow,
they know me, they name what I am
struggling with, they put into words
what I have been unable to find the
words for. Then put those few books
that have *really* affected you in a
bookcase close to where you work.
In my study I have all my favorite
books—my friends—just to the left
of my desk, in arm's reach. I have
lots more books in my study, but my
friends are right next to me.

• Interact with your books. Mark your
  favorite passages, make notes, mark

then file the quotes that grip you. Books are made to be marked and stained with tears, too. Reading is more than gathering information—it's a relationship.

- Don't worry if you take a break from reading now and then. Sometimes your soul needs space and time to process what's going on in your life. At such times reading can actually distract you from soul work you should be doing.

- Whatever you do, don't limit your reading to religious books. Read recent novels, old classics, biographies, short stories, essays, articles. Christians aren't the only ones speaking truth. Truth is truth, regardless of who says it.

- For what it's worth, here's my recommended reading list. Let it start you on the path to making your own book list.

Bob Benson, *Disciplines for the Inner Life* (Word)

Robert Benson, *Between the Dreaming & the Coming True* (Harper SanFrancisco)

Walter Brueggemann, *The Prophetic Imagination* (Fortress)

Thomas Cahill, *The Gifts of the Jews* (Doubleday)

Christopher DeVinck, *The Power of the Powerless* (Zondervan)

Jacques Ellul, *The Presence of the Kingdom* (Seabury)

Suzanne Farnham and others, *Listening Hearts* (Morehouse)

Arthur Gordon, *A Touch of Wonder* (Jove Books)

Thelma Hall, *Too Deep for Words* (Paulist)

Abraham Heschel, *Man's Quest for God* (Scribner's)

Abraham Heschel, *The Prophets* (HarperCollins)

Alan Jones, *Passion for Pilgrimage* (HarperCollins)

Alan Jones, *Soul Making: The Desert Way of Spirituality* (Harper SanFrancisco)

Thomas Kelly, *A Testament of Devotion* (Harper SanFrancisco)

Sue Monk Kidd, *When the Heart Waits* (HarperCollins)

Anne Lamott, *Traveling Mercies* (Pantheon)

Thomas Merton, *Thoughts in Solitude* (Noonday Press)

Johannes B. Metz, *Poverty of Spirit* (Paulist)

Kathleen Norris, *Amazing Grace: A Vocabulary of Faith* (Riverhead)

Kathleen Norris, *The Cloister Walk* (Riverhead)

Kathleen Norris, *Dakota: A Spiritual Geography* (Houghton Mifflin)

Henri Nouwen, *In the Name of Jesus* (Crossroad)

Henri Nouwen, *The Inner Voice of Love* (Doubleday)

Henri Nouwen, *The Road to Daybreak* (Image)

Parker Palmer, *Let Your Life Speak* (Jossey-Bass)

Parker Palmer, *To Know As We Are Known* (Harper SanFrancisco)

Eugene Peterson, *The Contemplative Pastor* (Word)

Eugene Peterson, *Living the Message* (HarperCollins)

Eugene Peterson, *A Long Obedience in the Same Direction* (InterVarsity Press)

Eugene Peterson, *Subversive Spirituality* (Eerdmans)

Barbara Brown Taylor, *The Preaching Life* (Cowley)

Barbara Brown Taylor, *When God Is Silent* (Cowley)

Evelyn Underhill, *The Spiritual Life* (Morehouse)

Evelyn Underhill, *The Ways of the Spirit* (Crossroad)

Dallas Willard, *The Spirit of the Disciplines* (Harper SanFrancisco)

Phillip Yancey, *The Jesus I Never Knew* (Zondervan)

Phillip Yancey, *What's So Amazing about Grace?* (Zondervan)

STOP IMPERSONATING YOURSELF.

Youth ministry is glittering image, full of highly visible programs, activities, and life-changing experiences. This makes it easy for youth ministers to dazzle parents and church members with their impact on young people. If you aren't careful, though, you *become* your program—fun, busy, energetic, passionate about God, confident—but with an inner life that is teem- i n g with insecurities, doubt, and struggles with your faith. If truth is at the center of the gospel, then truth must also be at the center of *you.* If teenagers are demanding reality today (and they are), then reality starts with you.

- Admit your own brokenness. Not that you have to publicly list all your sins, but you must somehow admit to your own sinfulness and flaws. If you want your students to feel safe in youth group, they need to know they're safe, flaws and all.

- Don't be afraid to admit your own struggles and doubts. What your students will hear is not disappointment that you struggle, but recognition of your faith in the middle of struggle and doubt.

- Humility is the first sign of genuine faith. Too many youth workers talk down to young people, bludgeoning them with "You need to do this" and "Unless you do that." They invariably use themselves as examples of commitment and dedication—despite the words of John the Baptizer: "He must increase, but I must decrease." Your job is not to impress young people with how spiritual you are, but with how faithful Jesus is. Your remarks about Jesus should always be sprinkled with gratitude.

- *Listen* to what your students tell you about their walk with Jesus. Don't teach them as if you're the only source of knowledge. Young people have much to teach *you* about Jesus.

- The call of youth ministry is all about Jesus. Your passion and desire should be to constantly bring people to Jesus.

THE CLOSER YOU GET TO JESUS, THE LESS YOU KNOW.

When I was 20, I knew everything about Jesus. I swaggered into high schools afraid of no one's arguments. The Bible was true, Jesus was God, and we all needed him.

I still believe those things, but the swagger is more like a limp now. I know Jesus, but I don't know much about him. I love the Bible—it's even more true to me today than it was 37 years ago—but the truth I see now is much more complicated and mysterious. Jesus is very real to me, but he is also very elusive. Sometimes I wonder whether I'm following him or he's following me. Life has left its scars on me, my soul is thick and leathery, faded and torn, knocked around a lot. I'm not as sure about things as I used to be.

Yet here's the amazing part, the one absolute I cannot shake: Jesus. As many times as I have disappointed him, as often as I have run from him, he has not given up on me. Every time I turn around, he's there. Every time I run from him, he's there.

I don't know as much about Jesus as I used to, but I do know one truth for sure. He's closer.

National Youth Workers Convention

NYWC

A place where you and other youth workers can come together, worship, learn, and play.

Broaden your spiritual horizons

Discover 16 ancient practices—such as the Ignatian Examen, centering prayer, and Sabbath—and learn why these proven spiritual disciplines are as relevant today as ever. Author Tony Jones briefly explores the historical and theological context of each discipline, then shows you how to implement it. If you feel like something is missing in your spiritual life, this book will challenge you to think about your relationship with God in new ways.

The Sacred Way
Spiritual Practices for Everyday Life
Tony Jones
RETAIL $12.99
ISBN 0310258103

Would You Rather...?
RETAIL $9.99
ISBN 0310209439

Unfinished Sentences
RETAIL $9.99
ISBN 0310230934

Tough Topics
RETAIL $8.99
ISBN 031024109X

Have You Ever...?
RETAIL $9.99
ISBN 031022439X

Name Your Favorite...!
RETAIL $9.99
ISBN 0310241979

What If?
RETAIL $9.99
ISBN 0310207762

This is the fun part of youth ministry. The off-the-wall, best-selling *Quick Questions* series gets students talking and thinking. Compact so they go with you everywhere, these indispensable resources make spiritual discussions enjoyable.

How much time do you spend at a computer? And how
much of that time do you spend working with pictures for
newsletters, presentations, or your website? *Art Source 4.0*
can make your print and electronic communication look
great with more than 2,000 images specifically for youth
ministry. Included are color clip art, borders, and web
elements.

ArtSource 4.0 CD-ROM
More than 2,300 Youth-Group-Specific Images
for Every Imaginable Ministry Use!

RETAIL $59.99
ISBN 0310257603

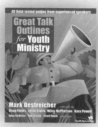 

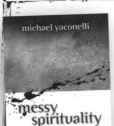

Messy Spirituality
God's Annoying Love for
Imperfect People

Michael Yaconelli

RETAIL $14.99
ISBN 0310235332

Devotion
A Raw-Truth Journal on
Following Jesus

Michael Yaconelli

RETAIL $10.99
ISBN 0310255597

In *Messy Spirituality*, Mike Yaconelli encourages us to invite God
into our lives—which will more readily lead to an authentic
relationship with him as opposed to white-knuckling ourselves
into the delusion that we first have to be okay before God
accepts us. The result? Not perfect people, but people perfectly
aware of the grace that God offers us every day of our lives.
Also, check out *Devotion*, a 30-day journal for your students, by
Mike Yaconelli.